T0401016

discovermore
Marine Wildlife

Crustaceans

Kaitlyn Salvatore

IN ASSOCIATION WITH

Published in 2025 by Britannica Educational Publishing (a trademark of Encyclopædia Britannica, Inc.) in association with The Rosen Publishing Group, Inc.
2544 Clinton Street, Buffalo, NY 14224

Distributed exclusively by Rosen Publishing.
To see additional Britannica Educational Publishing titles, go to rosenpublishing.com.

Editor: Brianna Propis
Book Design: Michael Flynn

Photo Credits: Cover Lynne2509/Shutterstock.com; (series background) Dai Yim/Shutterstock.com; p. 5 (top) Igor Kovalchuk/Shutterstock.com; p. 5 (bottom) Lynne2509/Shutterstock.com; p. 6 RLS Photo/Shutterstock.com; p. 7 Rattiya Thongdumhyu/Shutterstock.com; p. 8 https://commons.wikimedia.org/wiki/File:Tanaissus_lilljeborgi.jpg; p. 9 COULANGES/Shutterstock.com; p. 10 Anton Kozyrev/Shutterstock.com; p. 11 Vaclav Matous/Shutterstock.com; p. 12 Tarpan/Shutterstock.com; p. 13 Vladimir Wrangel/Shutterstock.com; p. 14 Choksawatdikorn/Shutterstock.com; p. 15 Mauro Rodrigues/Shutterstock.com; p. 16 RLS Photo/Shutterstock.com; p. 17 Solodov Aleksei/Shutterstock.com; p. 18 EcoPrint/Shutterstock.com; p. 19 Desi P/Shutterstock.com; p. 20 Ajit S N/Shutterstock.com; p. 21 (top) Wuttichok Panichiwarapun/Shutterstock.com; p. 21 (bottom) KIRYAKOVA ANNA/Shutterstock.com; p. 23 (top) Alexisaj/Shutterstock.com; p. 23 (bottom) Monir Morshed Khan/Shutterstock.com; p. 24 WoodysPhotos/Shutterstock.com; p. 25 LELACHANOK/Shutterstock.com; p. 26 Peter Zackariasson/Shutterstock.com; p. 27 divedog/Shutterstock.com; p. 28 one pony/Shutterstock.com; p. 29 TR STOK/Shutterstock.com.

Library of Congress Cataloging-in-Publication Data

Names: Salvatore, Kaitlyn, author.
Title: Crustaceans / Kaitlyn Salvatore.
Description: Buffalo : Britannica Educational Publishing, an imprint of Rosen Publishing, 2025. | Series: Discover more: marine wildlife | Includes bibliographical references and index.
Identifiers: LCCN 2024027729 | ISBN 9781641903516 (library binding) | ISBN 9781641903509 (paperback) | ISBN 9781641903523 (ebook)
Subjects: LCSH: Crustacea--Juvenile literature.
Classification: LCC QL437.2 .S25 2025 | DDC 595.3--dc23/eng/20240627
LC record available at https://lccn.loc.gov/2024027729

Manufactured in the United States of America

Some of the images in this book illustrate individuals who are models. The depictions do not imply actual situations or events.

CPSIA Compliance Information: Batch #CWBRIT25. For further information contact Rosen Publishing at 1-800-237-9932.

Contents

Crustacean Crew

Crustaceans are a large group of invertebrates. Crabs, lobsters, shrimp, and barnacles are some of the most recognizable crustaceans, but the group also includes many other lesser-known forms. In fact, there are around 45,000 species, or types, of crustaceans.

The word "crustacean" comes from the Latin word *crusta*, meaning "shell." Crustaceans have a hard but flexible outer shell called an exoskeleton and two pairs of antennae, or feelers, attached to their head. Crustaceans usually live in water. However, these animals have many different sizes, features, and habitats.

Do you know which kind of crustacean this is? It's a lobster!

compare and contrast

Crustaceans aren't the only animals with shells. Other animals, including armadillos and turtles, have shells too! What do you think are some similarities between a shrimp's shell and an armadillo's shell? What are some differences?

Crustaceans can't grow in the same way as other animals because their shells don't grow. So, instead, they must shed their shells and grow new ones. This is called molting!

From Big to Small

Crustaceans vary greatly in their shapes and sizes. The heaviest crustacean is the American lobster. It can reach a weight of 44 pounds (20 kg). The longest crustacean is the giant Japanese spider crab. Its legs can stretch up to 12 feet (3.7 m). Other crustaceans can be very large too. The Tasmanian giant crab can weigh as much as 31 pounds (14 kg). The average weight of the Alaskan king crab is 10 pounds (4.5 kg), but it can grow to over 20 pounds (9 kg).

Most American lobsters are rusty brown, but some are bright blue or blue green.

This is a water flea. It would only take up the space of a tiny corner of your fingernail!

At the other end of the scale, water fleas, fairy shrimp, and brine shrimp are some of the smallest crustaceans. Most are shorter than 0.25 inch (6.4 mm). Water fleas may only grow to be 0.009 inch (0.23 mm) long. Although they're tiny in size, water fleas serve as an important food source for many freshwater fish.

Consider This

New species of crustaceans are still being discovered by scientists. Why might species of crustaceans be hard for humans to find?

Underwater Homes

Crustaceans live in bodies of water throughout the world, including oceans, seas, lakes, and rivers. They can be found in fresh water, seawater, and inland **brines**. Some swim in open waters. Other species live at the bottom of the sea. Rocky, sandy, and muddy areas are all homes to crustaceans. Moreover, crustaceans can be found from the Arctic to Antarctic areas of the world.

Crustaceans called amphipods can live in ocean trenches more than 5.5 miles (8.9 km) deep, while water fleas can live in mountain lakes that are as much as 3 miles (4.8 km) above sea level.

Tanaids like this one are bottom dwellers. They live in shallow waters or the deep ocean. They feed on algae and bacteria.

Unlike most crabs, the European green crab can survive outside water for at least a week.

Some crustaceans are amphibious. That means they can live both on land and in water. Certain kinds of crabs and woodlice are amphibious.

WORD WISE

BRINES ARE NATURALLY OCCURRING SOURCES OF WATER WITH A VERY HIGH AMOUNT OF SALT IN THEM.

Segments and Body Parts

Crustaceans are a giant group of **arthropods**. The basic crustacean body is usually made up of segments, or sections. The exoskeleton covers each segment to protect the crustacean from harm.

At the front end of the body is a region called the acron. This is the head, or part of the head, on most crustaceans. At this end, adult crustaceans often have antennae pointing from the top-front area of the head and mandibles, or jaws that extend from their mouths.

About 80 percent of the animals on Earth are arthropods!

Like lobsters and crabs, crayfish, pictured here, have strong pincers.

Several pairs of limbs grow from the middle section of the body. Many species have different types of limbs for walking, swimming, or mating. Some species, including types of lobsters and crabs, have limbs with pincers, or claws.

WORD WISE

ARTHROPODS ARE A LARGE GROUP OF INVERTEBRATES THAT HAVE AN EXOSKELETON. INSECTS ARE THE LARGEST ARTHROPOD GROUP.

The abdomen, or tail end, of a crustacean is very different depending on the species. In many kinds of crustaceans, such as crabs, the tail is short. In some, such as lobsters, it may be as long as the rest of the body.

One to four pairs of small legs called swimmerets may be located on the underside of a crustacean's abdomen. Swimmerets are used for swimming, breathing, carrying eggs, and other functions.

Krill use gills in their legs to breathe in oxygen from the water.

A crustacean's tail may also help protect it from harm! For example, a lobster will dart backward by curling and uncurling its tail to escape from a predator while keeping an eye on the predator's whereabouts.

Larger species of crustaceans breathe using gills. Even crustaceans that live on land need gills to breathe. Smaller crustaceans do not require gills. Gases that move across the surface of their body through a process called diffusion keep them alive.

Crabs that live out of water use gills to breathe, but they must always keep their gills moist, or wet. How might they do this?

Different Groups

Copepods are one main group of small crustaceans. These are usually bottom-dwelling forms of zooplankton, which are tiny floating animals. Most crustaceans that are **parasites** are copepods. They commonly attach themselves to fish. Some copepods are an essential food source for marine (seawater) organisms, including many different kinds of whales.

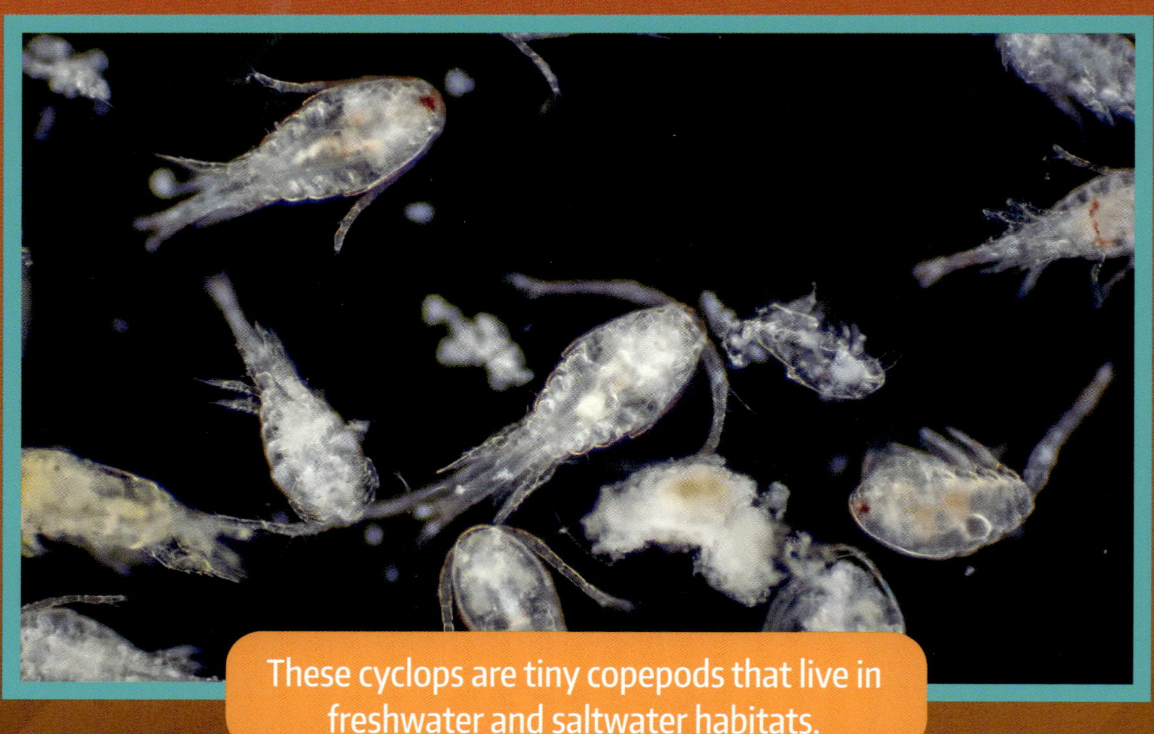

These cyclops are tiny copepods that live in freshwater and saltwater habitats.

A pill bug curls into a ball when it feels it's in danger.

Ostracods, or seed shrimp, are tiny marine or freshwater crustaceans. Their flattened shells give them the appearance of clams. Most live near the sea bottom. They are omnivores, which means they eat both plants and animals. They are also scavengers, eating dead creatures and waste.

The group of crustaceans called isopods has mostly marine forms, but the group includes the land-living sow bugs and pill bugs, or wood lice. Isopods are flat, usually gray, and have dozens of sharp claws on their undersides.

WORD WISE

PARASITES ARE ORGANISMS THAT LIVE ON OR INSIDE ANOTHER ORGANISM AND BENEFIT FROM IT BY RECEIVING FOOD, PROTECTION, OR BOTH IN A WAY THAT HARMS THE HOST.

Amphipods are a crustacean group closely related to isopods. This group is also mostly marine, and members often look like small shrimp. Amphipods that live on sand beaches are also called sand hoppers or sand fleas. Amphipods are important food for many animals, including fish, penguins, and seals.

These amphipods live underwater on a rock in the St. Lawrence River.

Amphipods have been found at depths of more than 30,000 feet (9,100 m)!

Barnacles are mostly marine crustaceans. Adult barnacles remain in one spot throughout their lives. They attach to any solid surface, including rocks, the underside of ships, and even turtles. Some species of barnacles are parasites in crabs and other crustaceans. Barnacles are filter feeders. This means they strain, or remove, plankton from the water that swirls around them.

The most important crustaceans to humans are the decapods. Many of these crustaceans are valuable sources of food. Lobsters, crabs, shrimp, and crayfish are decapods. Decapods are usually omnivores.

Consider This

In Alaska, a person can only catch Alaskan king crabs during certain times of year, and they are not allowed to take crabs of certain sizes or any female crabs. Why might this be?

Molt and Grow

Chitin, a hard protein substance, is the material that makes up a crustacean's exoskeleton. It protects the body and provides a place for muscles to attach. The thickness of the exoskeleton can range from very thin, as in some copepods, to a rigid—or unflexible—shell, as in crabs.

Crustaceans aren't the only arthropods with exoskeletons made of chitin—insects, scorpions, and other creatures have them too!

This molted crab exoskeleton could easily be mistaken for a resting crab!

Crustaceans molt, or shed, their exoskeletons several times as they grow. First, the old exoskeleton separates from the body. Then, new cells form the new exoskeleton. The old exoskeleton splits and is shed wholly or in parts.

Different species molt a different number of times from when they are born to adulthood. An adult crustacean may continue to molt, but it does not occur as often.

Consider This

Crabs that have lost legs can regrow them slowly through a series of molts. Can you think of any other animals that can regrow lost limbs?

Danger Ahead

While many crustaceans are predators, they all still face danger from other—and bigger—kinds of predators. Some crustaceans are eaten by fish and octopuses. Free-floating zooplankton are eaten by fish and larger marine animals, including whales. Birds eat crabs and other crustaceans.

Crustaceans have developed several adaptations for predatory protection. Some have colors or patterns that help them blend in with their habitat. Others burrow into the ground to avoid being found. Pill bugs roll themselves into tiny balls for protection.

Decapods with front pinching claws, such as lobsters and crabs, use these body parts to fight predators and to acquire food.

Blue whales—the largest animals on Earth—feed almost only on krill. Some eat up to six tons (5.4 mt) of krill a day!

Male fiddler crabs hold their large claw like a musician holds a violin or fiddle.

compare and contrast

Male fiddler crabs and ghost crabs grow one claw much larger than the other. What might be different about the way they find food or protect themselves compared to other crustaceans?

Emerging from the Egg

The reproduction and development of a crustacean from egg to adult is highly complex, or has many parts. The males usually have certain appendages used in the reproductive process. The females of most species carry their eggs on their body in some manner. Some female crustaceans, however, release their eggs into the water.

Some crustaceans hatch into a larva called a nauplius that does not look like an adult. Its body has only one segment and three sets of appendages. A nauplius's body changes with each molt.

Other crustacean young leave their eggs looking like adults. This is true for most isopods and amphipods, as well as for some decapods like freshwater crabs and crayfish.

Barnacles begin life as tiny zooplankton called nauplii. They begin changing into adults after attaching to a solid object by using a very strong glue-like substance made in their body.

compare and contrast

Barnacles usually have both male and female reproductive organs. Why do you think this is helpful for barnacles, compared to other crustaceans?

A female red crab can lay up to 100,000 eggs, which she holds in her abdominal sac.

Helping the Environment

No matter their size, all crustaceans play a key role in their respective food chains. They help keep ocean life balanced by eating plants and animals (alive or dead) or by being the food of larger animals. Without crustaceans, the careful balance of the food chain would be messed up.

More than 7.9 million tons (7.2 million mt) of crustaceans are harvested per year by fishers or farmers for human meals.

Some crabs, such as the Japanese spider crab seen here, clean the bottom of the ocean by eating dead animals. They also feed on mollusks and plants.

Crustaceans are very useful to humans. For instance, scientists have learned a lot about genetics by studying the genes of water fleas. Shrimp shells can be used to make an environmentally friendly plastic. Barnacles are crushed and used as fertilizer. Brine shrimp and water fleas are used as fish food in aquariums, and hermit crabs are popular pets. Crustaceans are also an important source of food for humans. Crabs, lobsters, and shrimp are popular menu items in restaurants and in markets worldwide.

Consider This

What would happen if humans began harvesting and eating crustaceans at a greater rate? How would this affect underwater food chains?

Pesky Parasites

While they are helpful to the environment, or natural world, crustaceans can also cause problems. Parasitic crustaceans get their food from their host while harming it. Some parasites may also pass deadly illnesses on to their host.

The amphipods nicknamed "killer shrimp" have become an **invasive species** in many lakes and rivers in Europe. The killer shrimp kill water creatures and then often do not even eat them.

Look at all the barnacles on the bottom of this sailboat! Workers will scrape, clean, and coat the bottom of the boat with paint.

European green crabs are an invasive species causing problems in Alaska. Their large appetites have left native species with no food and a fierce predator. They can also destroy eelgrass beds that are important to the environment.

Crustaceans can mean trouble for farms. Burrowing crabs drain water from rice paddies, exposing the roots of the plants to the sun. Land crabs and crayfish can harm tomato and cotton crops.

Large groups of barnacles cause damage, or harm, to ships and can reduce the speed of the ships through water. The shipping industry is continuing to find ways to control barnacles.

WORD WISE

AN INVASIVE SPECIES IS A NON-NATIVE SPECIES WHOSE INTRODUCTION TO AN ENVIRONMENT CAUSES HARM TO THE ECOSYSTEM AND THOSE ALREADY LIVING THERE, THREATENING THE BALANCE OF THE ECOSYSTEM ALTOGETHER.

Protection of Crustaceans

Whether they're food for other underwater animals or food for people, crustaceans are important animals in their ecosystems—meaning their health is important for both their habitats and for humankind. However, human activities threaten crustacean survival. One problem is overfishing. Countries have begun to put rules in place to stop people from catching too many crustaceans, which would cause the crustacean population to decrease.

Lobsters are caught in traps known as lobster pots. Fishermen usually bait the traps with dead fish to lure, or draw in, the lobsters.

Levels of carbon dioxide in the atmosphere have increased in recent years, and it will only continue to increase if humans do not change their habits.

Another threat to crustacean populations is fossil fuel emissions. When people burn fossil fuels for energy, a gas called carbon dioxide is released into Earth's atmosphere. Carbon dioxide also spreads into ocean waters, resulting in an increase in the ocean's acidity. Scientists have discovered that the increased acidity makes it harder for crustaceans to form their exoskeletons, which are important to their survival. Changes in human behavior are needed to protect crustaceans, or else the future of crustaceans and those that depend on them for food is uncertain.

Consider This

Fossil fuels—including oil, coal, and natural gas—are a source of energy for people. What other sources of energy can people use that wouldn't hurt the environment?

Glossary

adaptation A change in an organism or its parts that fits it better for the conditions of its environment.

appendage A body part (such as an arm or a leg) connected to the main part of the body.

burrow A hole in the ground made by an animal for shelter or protection. Also, to make a hole in the ground in which to live or hide.

ecosystem A community of living things interacting with their environment.

fertilizer A substance such as manure or a chemical used to make soil produce larger or more plant life.

flexible Capable of being bent.

fossil fuel A fuel (such as coal, oil, or natural gas) that is formed in the earth from plant or animal remains.

genetics The study of how features pass from parents to their young.

gill One of the filters on the side of an animal's body that are used for breathing.

habitat The place or type of place where a plant or animal naturally or normally lives or grows.

insect A small, six-legged animal with a three-part body.

invertebrate A creature that has no backbone.

mollusk Any of a large group of invertebrate animals (such as snails, clams, and octopuses) with a soft body lacking segments and usually enclosed in a shell containing calcium.

predator An animal that lives by killing and eating other animals.

protein Any of numerous substances that consist of many compounds essential for life and that are supplied by various foods.

reproduction The process by which plants and animals produce offspring.

trench A long, narrow, steep-sided depression in the ocean floor.

For More Information

Books

Brundle, Joanna. *Crustaceans*. New York, NY: KidHaven Publishing, 2020.

Schuh, Mari C. *Lobsters*. Mankato, MN: Amicus Inc., 2021.

Sexton, Colleen A. *Crabs*. Minnetonka, MN: Kaleidoscope Publishing Inc., 2023.

Websites

Britannica Kids: Crab
kids.britannica.com/kids/rticle/crab/353009
Read more about one of the most recognizable crustaceans: crabs!

National Geographic Kids: Peacock Mantis Shrimp
kids.nationalgeographic.com/animals/invertebrates/facts/peacockmantisshrimp
Learn about a colorful crustacean called the peacock mantis shrimp.

Science for Kids: What Are Crustaceans?
www.youtube.com/watch?v=PJsGC4vCGpQ
Review amazing facts about crustaceans and their habitats!

Publisher's note to educators and parents: Our editors have carefully reviewed these websites to ensure that they are suitable for students. Many websites change frequently, however, and we cannot guarantee that a site's future contents will continue to meet our high standards of quality and educational value. Be advised that students should be closely supervised whenever they access the internet.

Index